Published by Arcadia Children's Books
A Division of Arcadia Publishing
Charleston, SC
www.arcadiapublishing.com

Copyright © 2021 by Arcadia Children's Books • All rights reserved
First published 2021 • Manufactured in the United States
ISBN 978-1-4671-9817-2

Library of Congress Control Number: 2021932664

All rights reserved. No part of this book may be reproduced
or transmitted in any form whatsoever without prior written
permission from the publisher except in the case of brief
quotations embodied in critical articles and reviews.

All images used © Shutterstock.com; p. 15 Jason Sponseller /
Shutterstock.com; p. 24 Juli Scalzi / Shutterstock.com; pp. 28-29
Joe Hendrickson / Shutterstock.com; p. 30 James Marvin Phelps
/ Shutterstock.com; pp. 32-33 f11photo / Shutterstock.com; p. 36
Prosper106 / Shutterstock.com; pp. 40-41 Nina Alizada / Shutterstock.
com; pp. 56-57, 72 Eric Glenn / Shutterstock.com; pp. 58-59, 66-
67 Jason Sponseller / Shutterstock.com; pp. 76-77 Karl R. Martin
/ Shutterstock.com; p. 96 Harold Stiver / Shutterstock.com.

Cover illustration: Craig Yoe
Cover design: David Hastings
Page design: Jessica Nevins

Craig Yoe has written a TON of kids'
joke books! Yoe has been a creative
director for Nickelodeon, Disney, and
Jim Henson at the Muppets. Raised
in the Midwest, he has lived from
New York to California and has six kids!

CONTENTS

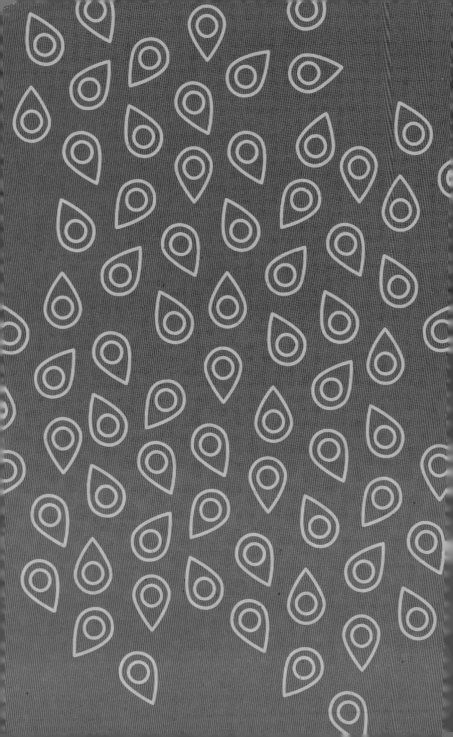

HOMETOWN HA-HAS

Did you hear the joke about Cleveland's tallest building, Key Tower?

No.

Never mind, it's over your head!

Key Tower

What starts with C and ends with E and has a million letters in it?

The Cleveland Post Office!

Where's the best place in Cleveland to exercise your tootsies?

Toe Path Trail!

Where do you live?

I live near Euclid Creek. Drop in anytime!

WHO'S THERE?!
Euclid!

EUCLID WHO?
Euclid open the door and find out!

FUN FACTOID

Holy Moses! The city of Cleveland is named after the city's founder Moses Cleaveland. The first "A" in Cleaveland was left out when a local newspaper didn't have enough room at the top of its front page, so "Cleveland" it is!

What's the best place in Cleveland to hang around?

University Circle!

What building in Cleveland has the most stories?

The Cleveland Public Library!

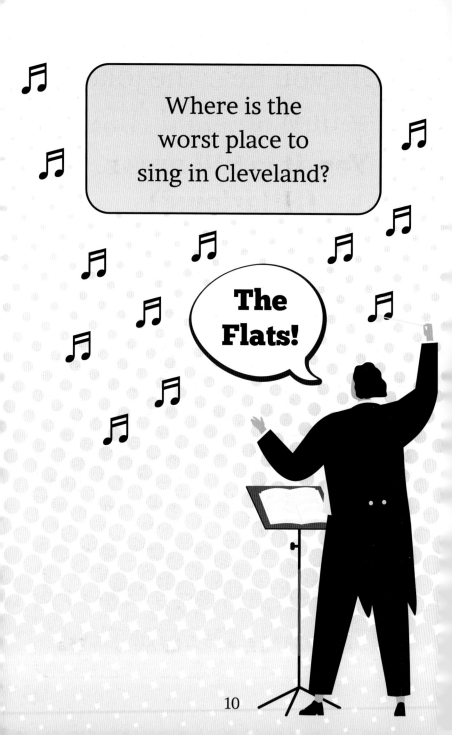

Did you hear the joke about Woodland Hills?

**Yes, it is hill areas!
(Hilarious!)**

Where does a mathematician
like to go in Ohio?

SUM-mit COUNT-y!

A LITTLE LIGHT HUMOR!

 LIGHT FACTOID

Cleveland had the first electric streetlights in the United States, first going up all the way back in 1879!

JIM:
STOP ME IF YOU HEARD THIS BEFORE! WHAT DID THE TRAFFIC LIGHT SAY TO THE FIRST PERSON WHO SAW IT?

TIM:
"DON'T LOOK AT ME, I'M CHANGING!"

BRIGHT FACTOID

The first ever electric traffic light was installed at the corner of Euclid Avenue and East 105th Street!

FUN FACTOID

You used to have to go to the post office to get your mail, but Joseph Briggs, a Cleveland postal worker, came up with the idea of home delivery in the early 1860s.

What did the letter say to the stamp?
"Stick with me, we'll go places!"

SK8 LAFFS AT CROOKED RIVER SKATE PARK

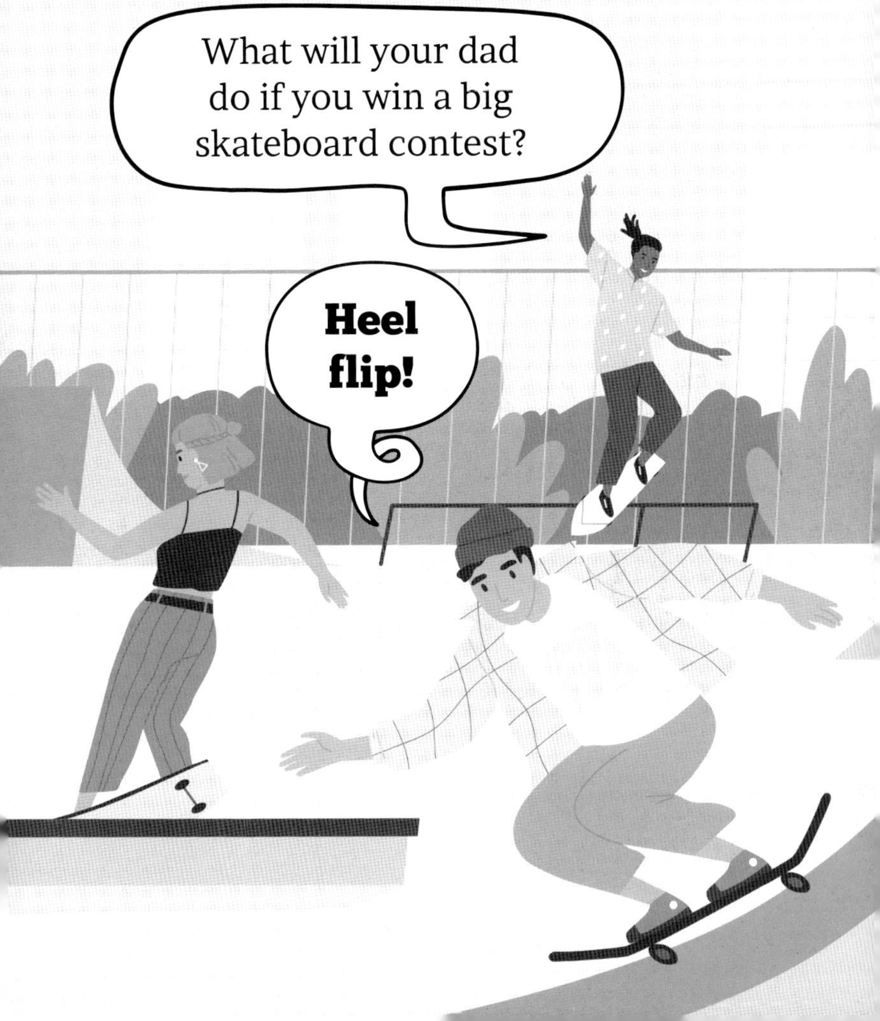

Let's visit the famous Cleveland comedy club, the Hilarities!

It's a hysterical landmark!

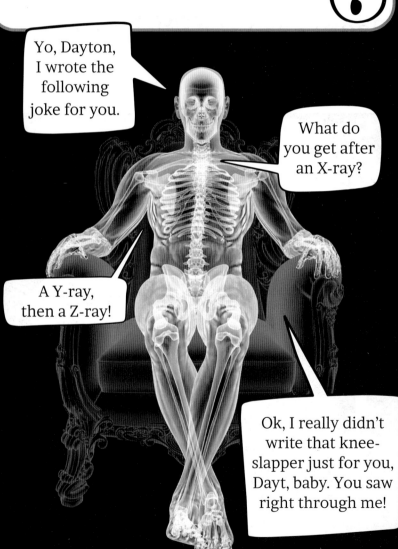

Why is there a fence around the Lake View Cemetery?

People are **DYiNG** to get in!

FROSTY FUN FACTOID

The house where the movie *A Christmas Story* was filmed is now a Cleveland museum!

It's located in the Tremont Neighborhood of Cleveland.

How can you tell that Santa is real?

You can sense his presents!

Superman was created in Cleveland by two teenagers. In honor of writer Jerry Siegel and artist Joe Shuster's creation, here are some Man of Steel jokes:

Why was Superboy the only kid playing at Cleveland Park?

Because the sign said, "Supervision Required!"

What's the difference between Superman and a fly?

Superman can fly, but a fly can't Superman!

What do you call Clark Kent when he sits down for dinner?

SUPPER-MAN!

What do you call Superman's toilet?
SUPERBOWL!

FUN FACTOIDS

 Located in Sandusky, Ohio (about sixty miles west of Cleveland), Cedar Point is the most-visited seasonal amusement park in the United States.

 Opened in 1870, Cedar Point is the second-oldest operating amusement park in the United States!

 Cedar Point has a world-record seventy-one rides, including seventeen roller coasters!

What did the orthodontist do when she went on Steel Vengeance?

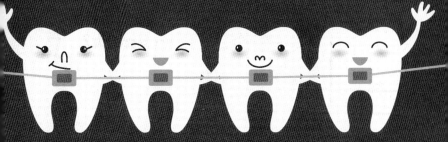

She braced herself!

Fun-lovers think Cleveland has the greatest theme park in the world!

I **SEE 'DER** POINT!

ROCK THESE JOKES AT THE ROCK & ROLL HALL OF FAME!

How does a chicken rock n' roller keep a beat?

With her drumsticks!

Wally: Did you hear about the band called the Beds?

Sam: No, tell me about them!

Wally: They mostly do covers!

ROCKIN' FACTOID

The term "rock n' roll" was made popular in the early 1950s by Cleveland DJ Alan Freed! ♫

What did the rocker say to the boulder?

ROCK ON!

Q: What did the drummer name her twin daughters?

A: Anna One, Anna Two...

ROCK & ROLL
HALL OF FAME

34

Ohio is the only state to have an official rock song. It's "Hang On Sloopy" by the McCoys!

George: What's a fish's favorite instrument?

Ringo: The bass drum!

Philip:
If University Circle married Public Square what would their baby be called?

Nicholas:
I dunno, but when the baby goes around, she'll have to cut corners!

"Judy's Hand" sculpture at Cleveland's Museum of Contemporary Art, July 2019.

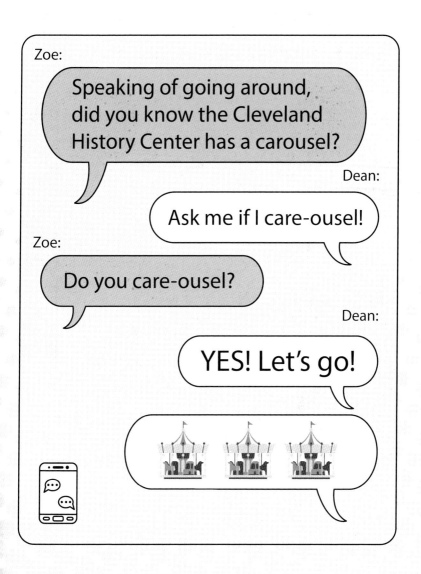

Zoe:

Speaking of going around, did you know the Cleveland History Center has a carousel?

Dean:

Ask me if I care-ousel!

Zoe:

Do you care-ousel?

Dean:

YES! Let's go!

37

CLEVELAND CLINIC CUT-UPS

The Cleveland Clinic is a world-famous medical center right here in Cleveland. In honor of the amazing professionals who save lives every day, here are the top-ten doctor and clinic jokes:

Why did the banana go to the Cleveland Clinic?
It wasn't peeling well!

What do you call two doctors?
Pair-o'-medics.

Doctor, doctor, I can't stop stealing things!
Come in and take a seat!

Doctor, doctor, I feel like a carrot!
Now don't get yourself in a stew

Why did the flashlight go to the Cleveland Clinic?
It was light-headed!

Doctor, doctor, every time I drink hot chocolate, I get a stabbing pain in my eye!

Next time, take the spoon out of the cup!

What did the doctor say to the patient who called to say he was invisible?

"Come into my office, and I'll see you!"

Why did the cookie go to the doctor?

He felt crumb-y!

Why did the pony go to the Cleveland Clinic?

It was a little hoarse!

And the number-one medical mirth joke...

Doctor, doctor, hurry, I'm shrinking!

Then you'll have to be a little patient!

BUCKEYE BANTER!

What's round on both ends and high in the middle?

☺HIO!

Where does Palpatine like to shop in Cleveland?

At the Darth Mall!

FUN FACTOID

Ok, there's not a Darth Mall in C-town, but in May 1890, the Arcade Cleveland opened as America's first indoor shopping center—the original mall, y'all!

What's in the middle of Cleveland?

The Letter "E!"

Fun Factoid

In the late 1890s, Clevelander Alexander Winton invented a truck that could deliver new cars to customers. It is widely considered to be the first the semi-truck in the world. In Alex's honor, we present a semi-funny joke:

What do you call a penguin in Cleveland?

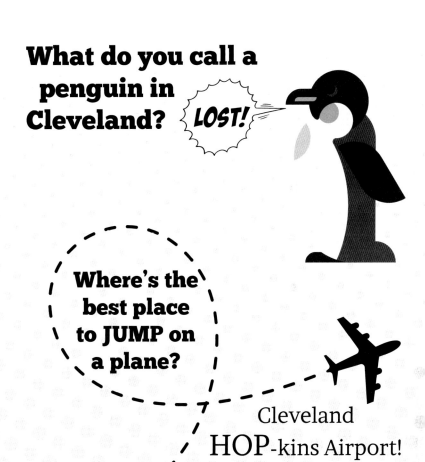

LOST!

Where's the best place to JUMP on a plane?

Cleveland HOP-kins Airport!

How did the flag feel at the Polish Constitution Day Parade?

Proud to be Pole-ish!

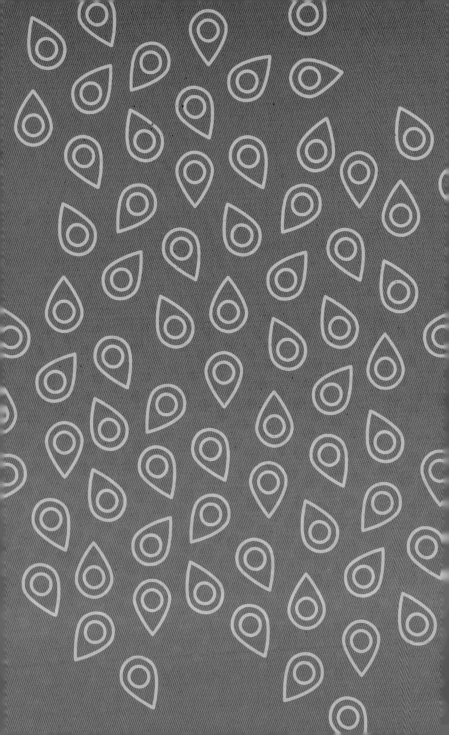

FUN FACTOID

Laugh your way to the bank! Cleveland has a money museum! It's sponsored by the Federal Reserve Bank of Cleveland and is a museum you could visit—for a change.

When the Children's Museum of Cleveland built their way-cool tree house, was it risky?

They did go out on a limb!

47

HIRE THIS GUIDE FOR THE SHAFRA PLANETARIUM:

Hello! My name is:

Skye Gazing

HIRE THIS GUIDE FOR FISHING AT ROCKY RIVER MARINA:

Hello! My name is:

Getta Polle

HIRE THIS GUIDE TO SHOW YOU THE CLEVELAND MUSEUM OF NATURAL HISTORY:

HIRE THIS GUIDE TO SHOW YOU THE CLEVELAND BOTANICAL GARDEN:

HIRE THIS GUIDE TO SHOW YOU THE CLEVELAND PUBLIC LIBRARY:

Hello! My name is:

Vera Literate

HIRE THIS GUIDE FOR THE CLEVELAND MUSEUM OF ART:

Hello! My name is:

Seymour Pikturz

HIRE THIS GUIDE TO SHOW YOU CLEVELAND'S BEST WORKOUT SPOTS:

Hello! My name is:

Jim Nastics

HIRE THIS GUIDE TO SHOW YOU THE CLEVELAND METROPARKS ZOO:

Hello! My name is:

Ellie Funt

♫ NOTE : ♫
CLEVELAND ORCHESTRA JOKES!

Why did Mozart get rid of his chickens?

Because they kept cackling, "Bach, Bach!"

Where did the Cleveland Orchestra conductor leave his keys?

In the piano!

What note did the cow keep playing?

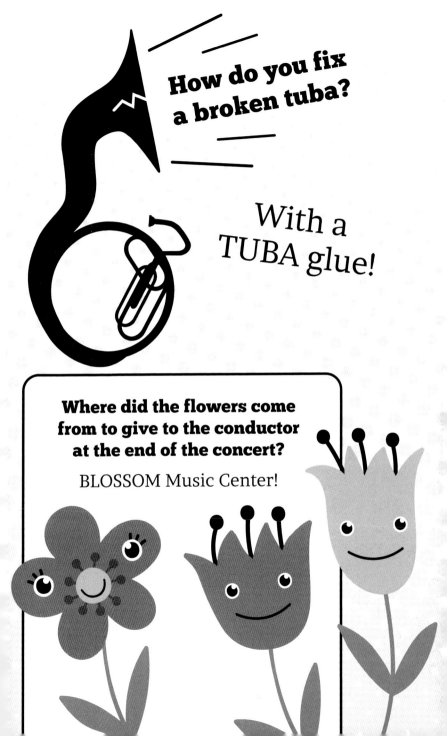

A DOG-GONE FUNNY JOKE TO TELL AT THE GREAT LAKES SCIENCE CENTER:

Great Lakes Science Center

ART-Y PARTY

Jokes to tell at the
Cleveland Museum of Art!

**Why did the pirate love
going to the CMA?**

He loved Arrrt!

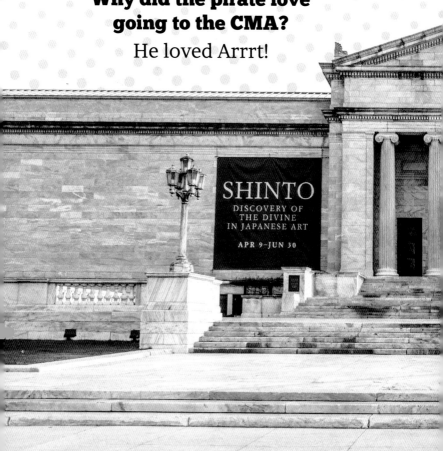

Tourist: Excuse me, can we take pictures?

Guard: No, you have to leave them on the wall.

What do you get when you combine Picasso with a Cleveland winter?

Ice Cubism!

Cleveland Museum of Art

NATURE JOKES

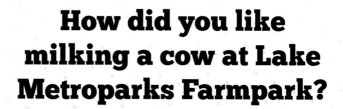

How did you like milking a cow at Lake Metroparks Farmpark?

It was a **MOO**-ving experience!

What did Lake Erie say to the lifeguard?

Nothing, it just waved!

Where does a ghost like to go for a walk on the beach?

Lake EERIE!

Customers at Mitchell's Ice Cream:

Where's the best place to buy syrup in C-town?

Maple Heights!

What did the boat say when it pulled up to the Edgewater Yacht Club?

What's up, dock?

Did you or your sister win the race up the shore at Edgewater Park Beach?

Neither, the race was **TiDE!**

Edgewater Park Beach

What did the sun bring to a party at Fairport Harbor Lakefront Park?

 A *LIGHT* snack!

READING A BOOK FROM THE CLEVELAND PUBLIC LIBRARY WHILE TANNING AT THE GENEVA MAKES YOU, WELL, RED!

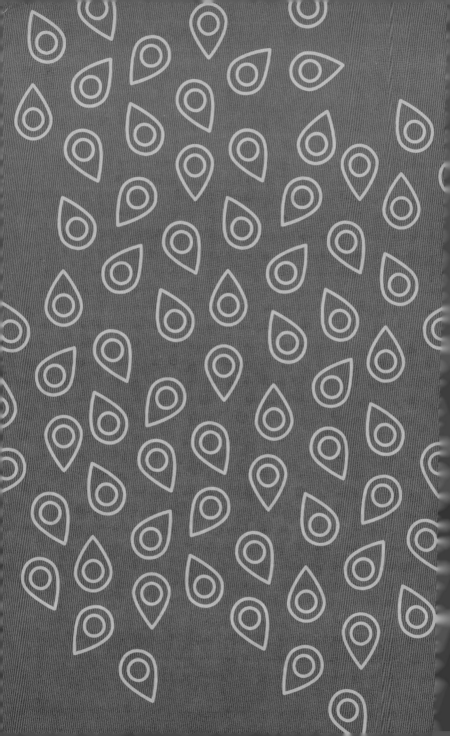

WHAT'S <u>ZOO</u> WITH YOU?

JOKES TO TELL AT THE CLEVELAND ZOO!

**Why is a giraffe such
a good father?**

Because he's someone
you can look up to!

**What has a tiger's stripes,
a porcupine's quills, and a rhino's horn?**

The Cleveland Zoo!

**How much money does the
skunk living in the Cleveland
Metroparks have?**

One scent

That
joke
stinks!

GREATER CLEVELAND AQUARIUM FISHY JOKES

75

FUN FACTOID

The Cleveland Metroparks celebrate a huge flock of buzzards that return from their winter vacation every year on March 15!

Here's a joke to tell the buzzards if you see them:

Cleveland Hopkins International Airport

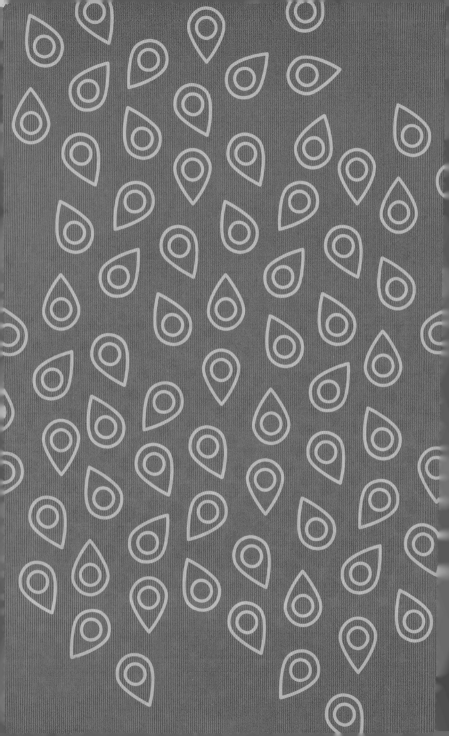

Clevelanders like to argue over which is the best mustard: Bertman Original Ball Park Mustard or Stadium Mustard! Let's bring the two sides together with a knee slapper...

Why did the vet put Bertman's on the dog with a fever?

Nothing is better than mustard on a hot dog!

CHOW DOWN ON THESE JOKES TO CELEBRATE THE FACT THAT CLEVELAND IS FAMOUS FOR ITS DELICIOUS POLISH FOOD!

Why did the baker stop making doughnuts and start making paczkis?
She was fed up with the HOLE thing!

Cleveland's "Polish Boy Sandwich"

Fiona:

I heard your brother got fired from the kielbasa factory!

Leo:

Yeah, he accidentally backed into the meat grinder and got a little behind in his work!

What kind of Polish food does a cat like?

A purrrrr-ogi!

FUN FACTOID

Yum! The bar is set high, but the largest candy store in America is in Cleveland! Sweeties has been selling candy for over sixty years. For all the customers at Sweeties, Griffin and Grace now present this sweet thought-provoking joke:

I bet you can't spell candy with two letters!

I sure can! **C and Y!**

FUN FACTOID

The first potato chip factory in the world was built in Cleveland on E. Seventy-Ninth Street by Cleveland farmer William Tappendon. He started making huge batches of potato chips and shipping them out to stores in 1895!

Why didn't the potato chip trust the sandwich?

Because the sandwich was full of baloney!

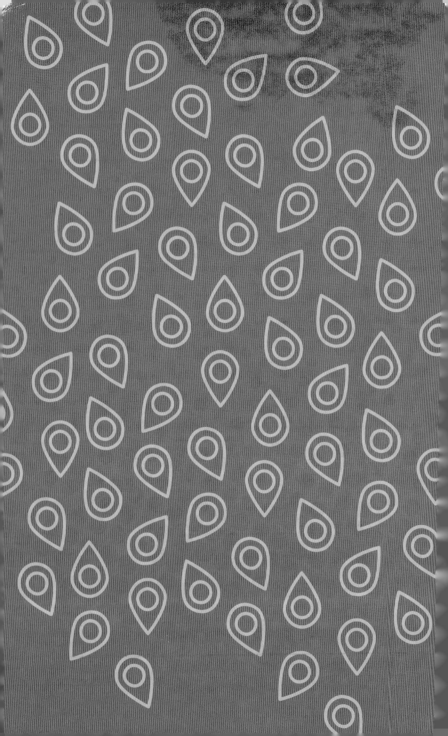

FUN FACTOID

Speaking of holes—as in golf—did you know the modern golf ball was invented by a guy in Cleveland in 1899?! Yup. Coburn Haskell invented the tightly wound rubber core that now sits at the center of every golf ball. That made them super bouncy, and golfers could hit them farther. Fore!

IN COBURN'S HONOR:

Why did Coburn Haskell wear two pairs of pants when he went golfing?

In case he got **a hole in one!**

Which Cleveland baseball player makes the best pancakes?

The batter.

What did the Cleveland outfielder's mitt say to the ball?

Why was the Cav's court wet?
The players **DRiBBLED** all over it!

Why couldn't the Cav go on vacation?

He got called for traveling!

Do you know what the enforcer on the Cleveland Monsters does?
Yes, of course!
Just checking!

What did the skeleton drive to the Cleveland Monsters' game?

A Zam-bony!

What position did the zombie try out for on the Monsters?

Ghoulie!

The bleacher section behind the Brown's end zone in FirstEnergy Stadium is affectionately called "the Dawg Pound!"

Which Cleveland Brown wears the biggest helmet?
THE ONE WITH THE BIGGEST HEAD!

FirstEnergy STADIUM